The Void Filler

Damon L. Morgan

The Void Filler

ISBN (Paperback): 978-1-960594-47-1
ISBN (Hardcover): 978-1-960594-48-8
ISBN (eBook): 978-1-960594-49-5

Published by Jacinth Media Productions LLC

Jacinthmediaproductions.com info@JacinthMediaProductions.com

Scripture quotations marked NASB are taken from the New American Standard Bible®, Copyright © 1960, 1971, 1977, 1995, 2020 by The Lockman Foundation. Used by permission.

Scripture quotations marked NIV are taken from the Holy Bible, New International Version®, NIV®. Copyright © 1973, 1978, 1984, 2011 by Biblica, Inc.™ Used by permission of Zondervan. All rights reserved worldwide.

Scripture quotations marked NLT are taken from the Holy Bible, New Living Translation, copyright ©1996, 2004, 2015 by Tyndale House Foundation. Used by permission of Tyndale House Publishers, Inc., Carol Stream, Illinois 60188. All rights reserved.

Scripture quotations marked ESV are from The ESV® Bible (The Holy Bible, English Standard Version®), copyright © 2001 by Crossway, a publishing ministry of Good News Publishers. Used by permission. All rights reserved.

Scripture quotations marked MSG are taken from THE MESSAGE, copyright © 1993, 2002, 2018 by Eugene H. Peterson. Used by permission of NavPress. All rights reserved. Represented by Tyndale House Publishers, Inc.

Scripture quotations marked NKJV are taken from the New King James Version®. Copyright © 1982 by Thomas Nelson. Used by permission. All rights reserved.

Scripture quotations marked CSB are taken from the Christian Standard Bible®, Copyright © 2017 by Holman Bible Publishers. Used by permission. Christian Standard Bible® and CSB® are federally registered trademarks of Holman Bible Publishers.

Printed in the United States of America

Contents

Dedication

This book is dedicated to **my village** without them there's literally no me in an earthly sense.

To **my wife**, who rocks out with me daily and during this with patience and faith - encouraged me to stick to it and get it done,

I love you my fine girl!

To **my children Drew, Taylor, Dylan**- your lives inspire me daily and daddy love you very much and my life is **committed to being an example for you all.**

To **my Mother (Ma Dukes)** words can't convey the appreciation, love and sacrifice you have made for me, your listening ear, your words of wisdom, advice and wisdom have shaped me!!

Love you mommy.

To **my Dad** and **Ma Barbara**, my bonus momma (I'm a blessed man) - I love you very much and thank you for loving on me, encouraging me and imparting in me inspiration and your love.

My Godmother who worked with my mom to get me where I am today. **Gina** I love you so much and your influence and presence helped me have the grit I have today. your belief in me and support of my authentic self never wavered.

To **my extended family aunts, uncles, sibling/cousins** (my cousins I call be and sis), **my in-loves** and **bonus family** whose presence shaped my growth thank y'all!!!

My Mentor - The Dr. Cedric Johnson, thank you and **momma V** for your continual relationship. It's not just about the pour but it's about the commitment to the mentorship. You took a young man who didn't care much for reading to now become one who enjoys a book here and there, lol. Thank you for showing the balance of thinking out the box while maintaining holy and holistic living while not getting distracted by the noise!!

And to **my late grandfathers**—your legacy of commitment, sacrifice, and purpose fuels my daily motivation. I endeavor to carry out your legacy all the days of my life as the Lord allows.

Foreword – *The Void Filler*

Every generation has to find new language for very old questions.

What do we do with our wounds?

Why do we feel empty even when our lives look full from the outside?

Where is God when the people and systems that were supposed to protect us end up wounding us instead?

The book you're holding, *The Void Filler*, is one person's attempt to tell the truth about those questions. It is not a systematic theology, nor is it a polished leadership manual. It is something more vulnerable and, in its own way, more demanding: a spiritual memoir written from the perspective of someone who has known both the ache of the void and the surprising nearness of God in the midst of it.

I have known Damon L. Morgan for more than fifteen years. We share roots in the Church of God in Christ, and I first noticed him not in a classroom or a ministry meeting, but behind a drum set – an exceptionally gifted young drummer serving at New York State denominational gatherings. As a drummer myself, his musicality caught my attention immediately, but it did not take long to see that there was more there than talent. Beneath the chops was a young man marked by deep spiritual hunger, genuine commitment, and integrity. What began as a musical mentoring relationship gradually unfolded into something more enduring: over time, the "drumming mentee" became a spiritual son.

I have watched Damon move through seasons of surrender, growth, and new responsibility. He was part of the core group that helped launch what would become the Kinetic Center, the faith-based creative arts collective I founded in Brooklyn. Today, he serves as our corporate treasurer, stewarding resources for a creative community committed to cultivating shalom in the lives of artists, activists, and everyday people.

That résumé matters, but it is not what qualifies him to write this book.

What qualifies him is that he has had to wrestle with his own brokenness, trauma, addiction, and longing for God, and he has chosen not to hide those struggles from others. When Damon writes about wounds, he is not writing as an observer. When he talks about masking pain behind a smile, he is not speaking in abstraction. When he names "the void," he is naming the interior spaces that many of us are taught to ignore or anesthetize.

In that sense, *The Void Filler* stands in the tradition of spiritual memoir and pastoral care. Damon is not simply telling a story about what happened. He is inviting readers to sit with their own stories, to slow down long enough to pay attention to the patterns, the lies we internalize, and the ways we try to manage our pain without actually healing it. Damon does this with a voice that is conversational, often poetic and direct. His language carries the cadence of testimony and the immediacy of a live conversation. As an emerging writer, he weaves story and Scripture together in ways that deepen rather than dilute the impact. That tension, between rawness and craft, is visible on every page. That is part of its gift.

Damon normalizes the presence of wounds without normalizing staying stuck in them. He does not glamorize brokenness, but he refuses to pretend that wholeness comes by way of denial. He takes seriously the role of secrecy, shame, and self-deception in keeping people from healing. You will read chapters that feel like a mirror held up to the ways we hide behind smiles, spirituality, and even ministry, while the unresolved void grows deeper underneath. Finally, he continuously returns to the conviction that God is not disgusted by our brokenness, but present in it, and committed to graciously filling what we cannot fill on our own.

There's an undeniable spiritual quality to Damon's voice. Some lines are jagged. But this is what makes his writing feel alive. He is speaking especially to those of us shaped by father wounds, institutional betrayals, or theological frameworks too narrow to hold our full humanity. Damon is reminding us that healing does not come through pretending, but through presence. Through showing up. Through crying out. Through learning how to fill the void not with performance or perfection, but with God. There are echoes of prophetic lament, moments of holy rage, glimpses of divine tenderness, and, at its core, an unmistakable undercurrent of hope.

Readers who come to this book expecting a quick fix will likely be disappointed. Readers who are willing to sit with honest questions will, I believe, find something more valuable – company. They will not find a disengaged expert, but someone who is likewise on a journey. And they will find language that may give them permission to tell the truth about their own story in ways they have not yet dared to speak aloud.

As someone who teaches, writes, and works at the intersection of counseling, pastoral care, and the lived realities of trauma and faith, I am always asking whether a given work contributes something real to the conversation. In Damon's case, I believe the answer is yes. Not because he has "figured it all out," but because he is willing to write with transparency from that liminal space in the middle – mid-journey, mid-struggle. That alone is an important witness in a Christian landscape that often prefers stories neatly tied up with a bow.

So I commend *The Void Filler* to you. Enter it with open hands and an open heart. Let it provoke you where it needs to. Use it in conversation with others, in small groups, in mentoring spaces where real talk is allowed. And as you do, I invite you to listen not only to Damon's voice, but to what the Spirit might be surfacing in your own life. In the very places that feel most empty, you may find the first quiet echoes of hope.

For pastors, counselors, small group leaders, or anyone mentoring someone through the long road of restoration, this book will be a gift. It gives flesh to grace, texture to transformation. And that, perhaps, is the most important contribution this book makes. It doesn't offer God as a vending machine or a magic wand. It offers God as *Emmanuel* – God with us, in the void, not afraid of the dark, and not in a rush to leave. In doing so, you may discover that the voids you carry are not simply evidence of what is missing, but places where God is already drawing near.

So read with openness. Read with honesty. And, if you can, read with the expectation that the One who fills the void may yet be at work.

Cedric C. Johnson, PhD
Associate Professor, John Jay College of Criminal Justice, CUNY
Founder & Director, Kinetic Center

Introduction

As a child, I developed a deep affection for puzzles. Among my favorites was a Teenage Mutant Ninja Turtles puzzle, though I must confess, I was also a huge fan of Legos. There was something uniquely satisfying about assembling a puzzle piece by piece; it sharpened my problem-solving abilities and focused my mind. But the real challenge came when a puzzle wasn't quite finished.

I remember one instance vividly: 95% of the puzzle was completed, but there was still one missing piece. Despite the nearly finished image, that single, absent piece left the puzzle looking incomplete, blank—almost ruined. The absence created a VOID—a void that left the puzzle appearing unfulfilled, even though everything else was seemingly in place.

I spent hours searching for that lost piece—sifting through my toy chest, discarding old toys, and rearranging things—until, finally, I found it. When I placed that last piece in its rightful spot, the puzzle was complete. And in that moment, I realized how much that missing piece had mattered. It wasn't just about filling a gap. It was about restoring wholeness.

It is amazing how the story of my puzzle parallels the essence of our lives. We are all, in some sense, on a quest to find that missing piece, that one thing we feel is absent—a void that needs to be filled. Life's challenges and shifting experiences often leave us searching for what will complete us. It's this VOID that seems to haunt us, a nagging emptiness that makes us feel incomplete, like something vital is missing.

A VOID is an empty space, a gap that demands to be filled. We search relentlessly to fill it—whether with relationships, success, possessions, or fleeting pleasures. Yet, no matter how much we try, these things only serve as temporary substitutes, promising satisfaction but never truly fulfilling our deepest desires. They may seem gratifying at first, but their ability to sustain us is limited. Eventually, we find that nothing the world offers, no material gain or fleeting pleasure, can satisfy the longing within us. The only thing capable of filling this void completely—and permanently—is Christ.

The absence of Christ in our lives is like a puzzle missing its key piece. Each of us carries a unique void, shaped by our background, our choices, our life experiences, and the unpredictable challenges we face. And while many things can offer temporary relief, nothing can restore wholeness except for Him.

I am writing this book from a place of deep reflection, not only for my own growth but also for the future of my children. As they grow older, I want them to understand that the ultimate key to fulfillment—what truly completes us—is Christ. Yes, we can experience happiness and success in life, but real fulfillment cannot be found without Him. Our lives can only reach their fullest potential when we allow Christ to fill the voids within us.

So, I invite you to join me on this reflective journey as we search together for that missing piece. It's time to discover the only thing that can fill the empty spaces we all experience—the key to true peace, joy, and lasting fulfillment. Come, let's begin the process of finding that puzzle piece, the one that completes us all.

IT STARTS SOMEWHERE...

It all began with curiosity in the garden. That ancient moment in Eden—the moment that redefined human history—wasn't just about fruit and temptation. It was about the deepest battle of the human heart: the choice between trusting God's Word or redefining truth on our own terms.

Genesis tells us that the serpent was "more crafty than any other beast of the field" (Genesis 3:1, ESV). His words were subtle, almost harmless on the surface, yet laced with the poison of doubt. "Did God *really* say...?" The question still echoes through time, infiltrating our own decisions. The tragedy of that first rebellion was not only the act itself, but the ripple effect—sin entered, communion was fractured, and humanity was displaced from its original state of Shalom.

In that one act, something was lost that we've been trying to recover ever since. It's what I call the *displacement ache*—that nagging sense that something vital is missing, that we were made for more but can't quite reach it.

The Anatomy of the Void

A void is not simply "nothingness." In Hebrew, the word *tohu* in Genesis 1:2 ("formless") conveys an emptiness that is not neutral but restless, yearning to be filled. In the human heart, the void is that restless space—the gap between what we are and what we were meant to be. We feel it when a dream is unfulfilled, when love is lost, when identity is shaken, or when our own failures seem to define us.

We try to fill it with substitutes: relationships, success, financial security, achievements, even religious activity. These may satisfy temporarily, but they cannot permanently silence the ache. As the writer of Ecclesiastes observed:

"He has planted eternity in the human heart..." (Ecclesiastes 3:11, NLT).

There is a God-shaped space within us, and as St. Augustine famously wrote, "Our hearts are restless until they find their rest in You."

The Cultural Reality

Today's culture excels at distraction. We are encouraged to mask pain with busyness, to numb our inner questions with entertainment, to curate an image rather than confront reality. But ignoring the void doesn't remove it—it deepens it.

I've seen it in friends, family, co-workers, and strangers:

The high achiever who collects awards yet feels unseen.

The devoted parent who sacrifices everything for their children but has forgotten who they are apart from that role.

The church leader who serves faithfully but inwardly battles burnout and bitterness.

Each is a variation of the same condition—living with a hollow space that nothing in this world can fill.

My Story—The Absence That Shaped Me

For me, the void took shape in my father's absence. Growing up in a single-parent home, I didn't have the constant presence of a dad to model manhood, to affirm my worth, to guide my choices. I saw my friends laugh and wrestle with their fathers while I went home to just my mom and my thoughts. That absence was more than emotional—it became formative.

Without realizing it, I began to construct a personality around pleasing others. If I could be the funniest, the most helpful, the most dependable friend, maybe I could earn the love I longed for. What I didn't understand then is what I know now: validation can never substitute for identity.

It took years before I could name what I was feeling. That hollow, restless ache wasn't just "loneliness"—it was the void. And the void is not neutral ground; it's contested territory. Left unaddressed, it becomes a breeding place for insecurity, comparison, and destructive coping mechanisms.

Scripture's Diagnosis

Romans 3:23 lays it bare: "For all have sinned and fall short of the glory of God" (NASB). That "falling short" is the very gap we feel. And here's the difficult truth: even our best self-effort can't close it. The prophet Jeremiah observed, "The heart is deceitful above all things, and desperately wicked; who can know it?" (Jeremiah 17:9, KJV).

Paul echoes this in *The Message* paraphrase of Romans 7: "I decide to do good, but I don't really do it; I decide not to do bad, but then I do it anyway." In other words, without divine intervention, we are stuck in a cycle of knowing better but doing worse—feeding the void instead of filling it.

The Turning Point—Accountability

Here's the thing about life: you cannot live it well without accountability. Accountability to God. Accountability to truth. Accountability to people who will tell you when you're drifting. Without it, we make reckless choices that multiply our emptiness.

 Viktor Frankl, in *Man's Search for Meaning*, wrote: "When we are no longer able to change a situation, we are challenged to change ourselves." Adam and Eve couldn't undo their choice in Eden, but they could (and did) start walking out the consequences. For us, too, the question becomes: Will I own my story, or will I keep blaming someone else for it?

The Call to Intention

Filling the void requires Spirit-led intentionality. The Holy Spirit becomes both the compass and the companion in this journey. And that means choosing every day—sometimes every hour—to reject the cheap substitutes and pursue the real thing.

That pursuit is costly. It may mean letting go of habits, places, or relationships that reinforce your emptiness. It may mean facing grief you've buried for years. But the cost of avoiding the void is far greater: a life half-lived, a soul never satisfied.

The Beginning of Restoration

It starts somewhere—in the garden, in a childhood wound, in a betrayal, in a dream deferred. The location varies, but the effect is the same: something sacred has been lost, and only the Creator can restore it.

This chapter isn't about shame; it's about recognition. If you can name your void, you're already on the path toward healing. And healing begins when we stop trying to fill it ourselves and invite the One who made us to fill it with His presence.

Because the truth is... left alone, the void only deepens. But surrendered to Christ, the void becomes the very place where His glory takes root.

MAYDAY! MAYDAY!#ENTANGLEMENT

We left Chapter 1 with the sobering realization that the void is real, it's personal, and if we leave it unaddressed, it only deepens. But here's the thing: once we recognize the void, we are often confronted by something even more unsettling—the methods we've been using to try to fill it.

And sometimes, that moment of recognition feels like being in a spiraling aircraft. The engine's failing, the oxygen mask drops, and all your training (or lack thereof) is about to be tested.

"Mayday! Mayday!"

It's the universal distress call for pilots in trouble. And in the spiritual life, we have our own Mayday moments—when the temptation is too strong, the habit too ingrained, the idol too comfortable to let go. These are the moments when we know we're in trouble, but pride, fear, or shame keep us from grabbing the radio and calling for help.

From Recognition to Crisis

In Chapter 1, we talked about the origins of the void. Now, in Chapter 2, we're looking at what happens when we try to fill that void with anything other than Christ. And let me tell you—the counterfeit fillers don't just fail; they entangle us.

James, the brother of Jesus, doesn't mince words:

"Let no one say when he is tempted, 'I am tempted by God'; for God cannot be tempted by evil, nor does He Himself tempt anyone. But each one is tempted when he is drawn away by his own desires and enticed. Then, when desire has conceived, it gives birth to sin; and sin, when it is full-grown, brings forth death." (James 1:13–15, NKJV)

Notice the sequence: drawn away → enticed → conceived → sin → death.

It's a progression. Temptation rarely drops on us out of nowhere; it starts with a desire. And if that desire is misaligned, unchecked, or rooted in a wound we refuse to address, it becomes the seed of our downfall.

The Seductive Power of the Idol

Let's call it what it is: behind every unchecked desire is an idol.

Now, in the Old Testament, idols were carved images—statues of Baal, Asherah poles, golden calves. Today, our idols might look shinier and smell better, but they still hold the same power to seduce, distract, and enslave.

For some, the idol is success—the constant chase for the next raise, the next title, the next applause.☐
For others, it's relationships—placing someone else at the center of our identity, making their approval our oxygen.☐
For many, it's a vice—pornography, alcohol, substances, gambling, or even compulsive shopping.

Carl Jung once said, "Every form of addiction is bad, no matter whether the narcotic be alcohol or morphine or idealism." That last word, *idealism*, hit me like a brick. Because here's the truth: you can even be addicted to a good thing—ministry, generosity, self-improvement—if you're using it to avoid the deeper issue.

My Idol: The Need for Validation

If I'm going to talk about idols, I have to confess mine. For years, my idol was the need for validation through women. I masked it as charm, flirtation, and "just being Damon," but underneath, it was a deep hunger for approval and control.

The pattern was predictable: meet someone, turn on the charm, work hard to win her affection, and then... leave. It wasn't about love; it was about the rush of being chosen. And once I was chosen, the thrill faded, and the void was still there.

Looking back, I see how that idol consumed me. It promised connection but delivered isolation. It whispered empowerment but left me powerless over my own impulses. And here's the kicker—it wasn't just damaging me; it was damaging others.

Pandemic Proof: The Idols Thrived

If you think idols only thrive in "normal" life, look at what happened during the COVID-19 pandemic. A multi-billion-dollar pornography industry saw massive spikes in usage as isolation set in. Substance abuse skyrocketed. Online shopping surged. Food delivery apps broke records.

Why? Because when we're cut off from our usual distractions, the void starts screaming louder. And if we don't run to Christ, we run to whatever will give us the fastest numbing hit.

But here's the problem: idols don't heal wounds. They only deepen them. They may offer a moment of relief, but they always demand a higher payment later—in our integrity, relationships, and peace.

Relational Entanglements

Let's be real. One of the most common arenas for idol-driven entanglement is relationships. When two people with unresolved wounds come together, the relationship becomes less about love and more about mutual anesthesia.

You expect them to complete you. They expect you to complete them. And because both of you are incomplete, the relationship quickly becomes a cycle of disappointment and resentment.

This is why Paul warned the Corinthians about being "unequally yoked" (2 Corinthians 6:14, AMP). It's not just about faith alignment; it's about wound alignment. If your wounds feed each other instead of healing each other, the entanglement will choke the life out of both of you.

The Transactional Trap

Unchecked idols eventually become transactional. They take on a generational life of their own. Your patterns become your children's patterns. Your coping mechanisms become their survival strategies.

This is why someone in the bloodline has to make the decision to break the cycle. Orrin Woodward said, "Self-denial in the pursuit of purpose generates true pleasure, while self-indulgence in the pursuit of pleasure generates true misery."

Self-denial isn't about legalism; it's about liberation. It's the willingness to let go of something that's killing you so you can grab hold of the life God has for you.

Breaking the Cycle

Breaking free starts with a decision. And that decision has to be backed by accountability, honesty, and a plan.

It might mean confessing the struggle to a trusted friend or mentor.□
It might mean deleting phone numbers, canceling subscriptions, or changing routines.□
It might mean—and usually does mean—asking the Holy Spirit to expose the root of the desire so it can be healed rather than just suppressed.

Because here's the truth: if we only manage the behavior without healing the wound, the idol will just change form and come back wearing a different mask.

From Mayday to Mission

If "Mayday" is the cry for help, then "Mission" is what happens when you land the plane and start living with purpose again. The shift from panic to purpose is not instantaneous; it's a process. But the first step is admitting the danger.

Sin loves secrecy. Idols thrive in the dark. The moment you bring them into the light—confessing to God, confessing to someone you trust—their power begins to weaken.

John writes:

"If we confess our sins, He is faithful and righteous to forgive us our sins and to cleanse us from all unrighteousness." (1 John 1:9, NASB)

That's not just forgiveness—that's cleansing. That's God not only forgiving what you've done but restoring what's been broken.

Mayday moments aren't just about identifying that you're in trouble; they're invitations to change course. But you can't just pull up on the yoke and hope for the best—you need a new flight plan, one authored by the One who knows the terrain of your heart.

Idols will always promise the quick fix. Christ will always promise the complete cure. The quick fix numbs; the cure heals.

The question is: which one will you choose?

Because if you keep running back to the idol, you'll find yourself digging in the same spot, looking for treasure that isn't there. But if you let Christ break the entanglement, you'll finally be free to start digging in the right place.

And that leads us straight into the next part of our journey... Treasure Hunting.

TREASURE HUNTING

We've sounded the Mayday. We've faced the entanglements. We've admitted that our idols—no matter how shiny, seductive, or soothing in the moment—cannot and will not heal us.

Now comes the inevitable question: If I'm not chasing that... then what am I chasing?

Because here's the truth—we were designed to seek. Every human being is on a hunt. The real question is: what are we hunting for, and where are we looking?

The Universal Search

Jesus boiled it down in Matthew 6:21 (NLT):
"Wherever your treasure is, there the desires of your heart will also be."

The Message paraphrase says it like this:
"It's obvious, isn't it? The place where your treasure is, is the place you will most want to be, and end up being."

Treasure is not just gold and jewels—it's whatever you believe will finally make you whole. For some, it's a career goal. For others, it's a relationship. For still others, it's financial stability, social influence, or personal freedom.

The problem isn't the desire itself—desire is God-given. The problem is when the object of that desire is misaligned. When our treasure is in the wrong place, our heart will be too.

Childhood Treasure Hunts

As a kid, I loved games that involved searching. Sometimes it was a scavenger hunt around the neighborhood. Sometimes it was combing the backyard for "buried treasure" that was really just a jar of coins I'd hidden from myself.

The thrill was in the pursuit—the clues, the chase, the hope that what I'd find would be worth the effort. But you know what's worse than coming up empty-handed? Finding the "treasure" only to realize it's not worth anything.

That's the story of so many lives: years spent searching, digging, sacrificing... only to hold in our hands something that looks like gold but crumbles like dust.

The Counterfeit Prize

The void inside us doesn't just want something—it wants something ultimate. When we attach that longing to anything other than God, we end up with what Jeremiah 2:13 (NIV) calls "broken cisterns that cannot hold water."

We work hard to get the relationship, but the relationship can't hold the weight of our soul.□
We climb the corporate ladder, but the view from the top isn't what we thought it would be.□
We buy the house, the car, the gadgets, but the new smell fades and the novelty dies.

Every counterfeit treasure has an expiration date. And here's the dangerous part—instead of re-evaluating the map, we just dig harder in the same place.

The Cost of Digging in the Wrong Place

Digging takes energy. It takes time. And every swing of the shovel into the wrong soil is time and energy you'll never get back. I've seen people spend decades chasing approval, image, or revenge—only to wake up exhausted and empty.

Haggai 1:6 (NASB) captures the feeling perfectly:
"You have sown much, but harvest little; you eat, but there is not enough to be satisfied; you drink, but there is not enough to become drunk; you put on clothing, but no one is warm enough; and he who earns wages earns wages to put into a purse with holes."

A purse with holes. That's the image of a life chasing treasures that cannot keep what they promise.

Leaving the Real You Behind

The more we dig in the wrong place, the more we lose ourselves. It's not just about wasted time—it's about misplaced identity.

I remember seasons in my own life where I was so wrapped up in the pursuit of something—or someone—that I didn't even recognize myself anymore. I wasn't Damon the son, Damon the friend, Damon the man of God in process. I was Damon the performer, Damon the charmer, Damon the achiever—always chasing, never arriving.

When you're living like that, the "real you" gets buried under layers of pretense. You're surviving, not thriving. And comfort zones—as nice as they feel—become prisons.

Roy T. Bennett said, "The comfort zone is a psychological state in which one feels familiar, safe, at ease, and secure. You can never change your life until you step out of your comfort zone. Change begins at the end of your comfort zone."

The comfort zone will let you keep digging in the wrong place without asking hard questions. Stepping out of it forces you to assess the map—and sometimes to admit that you've been chasing the wrong treasure altogether.

A New Map

The gospel offers us a new treasure map—and it's not a map to something, but to Someone.

Jesus told two short parables in Matthew 13:44–46 (AMP) that reveal the heart of the hunt:

"The kingdom of heaven is like a treasure hidden in a field, which a man found and hid again; then in his joy he goes and sells all he has and buys that field. Again, the kingdom of heaven is like a merchant in search of fine pearls, and upon finding a pearl of great value, he went and sold all he had and bought it."

Notice the joy. The man doesn't sell everything in bitterness; he does it gladly because he knows what he's getting is worth far more than what he's giving up.

This is where the hunt changes: when you realize that Christ Himself is the treasure, the sacrifices stop feeling like losses and start feeling like investments.

The Work of Filling the Void

But here's the honest truth—even when you find the true treasure, the work isn't over. You still have to guard it, value it, and resist the pull back to counterfeit gold.

For me, that meant doing some excavation in my own heart. It meant asking:

Where did I learn to equate love with performance?

Why did I believe that validation was something to be earned rather than received as a gift?

How much of my pursuit of "treasure" was really just a bid to silence the echo of my father's absence?

Those questions weren't comfortable, but they were necessary. Because until I could answer them, I was always at risk of wandering off the map again.

The Deep Treasure

C.S. Lewis famously wrote in *Mere Christianity*:

"If I find in myself desires which nothing in this world can satisfy, the most probable explanation is that I was made for another world."

That's it. The ache for treasure that lasts is proof we were made for more than this earth can offer.

Every pleasure here—even the good, God-given ones—is meant to point beyond itself to the ultimate treasure: intimacy with the One who made us. When we stop at the gift and ignore the Giver, we cheapen the hunt and rob ourselves of the joy that comes with finding the real thing.

Treasure hunting isn't wrong. The problem is when the map we're using leads us away from the true prize. Every wrong dig drains our energy and deepens the void. But every right step toward Christ fills it—not just partially, but completely.

In the next chapter, we'll deal with something most of us are experts at—smiling through the pain. Because even when we've found the treasure, we often hide the fact that we're still healing.

And that's where we'll talk about why "*This Smile is Hurting Me.*"

THIS SMILE IS HURTING ME

We ended Chapter 3 talking about the pursuit of treasure—that all of us are searching for something that will finally make us feel complete. But here's the twist: even when we find the true treasure in Christ, it doesn't mean the old wounds disappear overnight. Sometimes, we're still in the process of healing—still learning to walk in the reality of what we've found.

And in that in-between space, we often reach for a mask.

For some, the mask is busyness. For others, it's overachieving. For me—and for many—it has been a literal smile. Smiling through the pain. Keeping up appearances so no one asks too many questions. Pretending the treasure hunt is over and we're perfectly fine, when deep down we know the truth: *this smile is hurting me.*

The Mask and the Mirror

James says it with surgical clarity:

"But be doers of the word, and not merely hearers who deceive themselves. Because if anyone is a hearer of the word and not a doer, he is like someone looking at his own face in a mirror; for he looks at himself, goes away, and immediately forgets what kind of person he was." (James 1:22–24, CSB)

The mirror shows us reality. The mask hides it. And the longer we wear the mask, the harder it is to remember what's underneath.

Theologian Dietrich Bonhoeffer once wrote, "We must learn to regard people less in light of what they do or omit to do, and more in the light of what they suffer." Behind every mask is a story—and behind every smile is either genuine joy or silent suffering.

Makeup and the Illusion of Wholeness

My wife is a fan of MAC makeup. She's naturally beautiful without it (and yes, I've told her this many times), but I've watched the meticulous care she takes when applying it—blending, contouring, highlighting. It's an art.

The makeup industry is worth billions because it sells more than products—it sells the promise of enhancement, the idea that you can present your best self to the world. But the thing about makeup is... it's temporary. No matter how flawless the application, it all comes off at the end of the day.

Our emotional masks work the same way. They can enhance our public image, hide our insecurities, and project confidence we don't actually feel. But sooner or later, the mask comes off. And when it does, we're left face-to-face with the unfiltered version of ourselves.

What's Underneath the Smile

Under the mask could be any number of things:

Grief that you don't feel free to express because people expect you to be "over it" by now.

Shame from mistakes you've made that still whisper lies about who you are.

Anger that has calcified into cynicism because it's been unaddressed for too long.

Fear that if people really knew the truth about you, they'd leave.

Dr. Gabor Maté, in his work on trauma, says, "Trauma is not what happens to you. Trauma is what happens inside you as a result of what happens to you." That's why two people can experience similar events but process them in completely different ways—because the deepest wounds are not just in the event, but in the internal shift it causes.

Survival Mode

When you've been wounded, survival mode can feel like the only option. Keep moving. Keep smiling. Keep producing. Keep people at a safe distance.

The problem is, survival mode is meant to be temporary. If you live there too long, it becomes normal. You forget what real joy feels like because you've trained yourself to settle for the performance of joy.

That's where I found myself at one point—leading, serving, smiling, but internally fractured. I had convinced myself that pretending to be whole was the fastest route to becoming whole.

Spoiler: It wasn't.

Biblical Examples of Mask-Wearing

The Bible is full of people who wore masks—not literal ones, but facades to protect their image or avoid vulnerability:

King Saul put on the mask of confidence while being eaten alive by insecurity (1 Samuel 15).

Peter put on the mask of loyalty, swearing he'd never deny Jesus, only to crumble under pressure (Luke 22:54–62).

The Pharisees perfected the mask of religious performance, but Jesus called them "whitewashed tombs"—beautiful on the outside, but full of decay inside (Matthew 23:27, NIV).

Masks may protect you in the moment, but they rob you in the long run.

Why We Hide

We hide because exposure feels dangerous.⊓
We hide because admitting we're not okay feels like weakness.☐
We hide because we fear rejection more than we desire healing.

Adam and Eve, after sin entered, hid themselves among the trees. When God called out, "Where are you?" (Genesis 3:9, NKJV), it wasn't because He didn't know their location—it was an invitation to step out of hiding and into healing.

That same invitation stands for us today. God already sees beneath the mask. He already knows what's fueling the smile that's hurting you. The question is whether you'll let Him address it.

Triggers and Trauma Idols

One of the more subtle dangers of hiding is that our unaddressed trauma can become an idol. We nurse it, protect it, and even structure our lives around it.

Certain words, places, or situations trigger us, and instead of seeing those as opportunities for healing, we see them as reminders to build stronger walls.

But an idol—even if it's born from pain—still takes the place of God in our hearts. And no idol, no matter how justified we feel in having it, can bring the wholeness we crave.

The Courage to Unmask

Paul says in 2 Corinthians 3:18 (AMP):

"And we all, with unveiled face, continually seeing as in a mirror the glory of the Lord, are progressively being transformed into His image from [one degree of] glory to [even more] glory, which comes from the Lord, [who is] the Spirit."

Unveiled face. No mask. No makeup for the soul. That's the space where transformation happens—not in hiding, but in beholding.

Unmasking doesn't mean oversharing with everyone you meet. It means letting the right people into your process—trusted friends, wise mentors, counselors, and most importantly, the God who already knows.

Yes, the smile may be hurting you right now. Yes, taking off the mask feels risky. But staying hidden will cost you more than stepping into the light ever will.

The mask can protect you from immediate rejection, but it will also keep you from deep connection. And the only way to heal the void is to let the God who fills it see you as you are—and to let others in who can remind you of the truth when you forget it.

In the next chapter, we'll deal with what happens once you start unmasking—when you're finally ready to stop hiding and start dealing with the wounds themselves. Because healing isn't just about revealing the pain; it's about addressing it at the root.

DEALING WITH THE WOUNDS – THE SECRET DECEPTION

When the mask finally comes off, something happens. There's a moment of relief — the pretending is over. But almost immediately, there's also a moment of reckoning. Because now, you have to actually look at the wound you've been covering.

And if we're honest, some of us have been hiding those wounds for so long that we've mistaken the bandage for the cure. We've learned how to live around the injury instead of letting God heal it. That, my friend, is the secret deception — the belief that if we can just manage the symptoms, we can ignore the disease.

Paul's Confession of the Battle Within

Paul lays it out with gut-level honesty in Romans 7:18–20, 24 (NASB):
"For I know that nothing good dwells in me, that is, in my flesh; for the willing is present in me, but the doing of the good is not. For the good that I want, I do not do, but I practice the very evil that I do not want... Wretched man that I am! Who will set me free from the body of this death?"

This is the apostle Paul — the man who wrote most of the New Testament — admitting that there's a war inside him. He wants to do right, but the pull toward wrong is still there. That pull is often the exposed nerve of an unhealed wound.

The wound creates vulnerability. The vulnerability opens the door for temptation. And temptation, if entertained, leads us right back to the very behaviors we swore we'd left behind.

The Nature of Wounds

Not all wounds are created equal.

Some are inherited — passed down through family patterns, generational sin, or environmental dysfunction.

Some are inflicted — caused by betrayal, abuse, rejection, or abandonment.

Some are self-inflicted — the result of our own decisions, our own rebellion, our own stubbornness.

Regardless of the source, wounds that go untreated always deepen. A minor scrape can turn into a life-threatening infection if ignored. The same is true for the soul.

A Bike, a Fall, and the Lesson of Infection

When I was a kid, I rode my bike like it was my ticket to freedom. One day, I hit a rock I didn't see and went flying. My knee tore open. My mom cleaned it and bandaged it, but here's the thing — I didn't want to slow down. I wanted to get back on the bike.

Within days, the wound looked worse. It was swollen, hot to the touch, and painful. Why? Because I had been protecting the surface while still exposing it to dirt and bacteria. The bandage gave the illusion of safety, but the infection beneath was growing.

That's how many of us live spiritually and emotionally — slapping a quick fix over a deep injury and convincing ourselves it's handled. But just like my knee, the wound festers beneath the surface until it demands attention.

The Psychological Cost of Unhealed Wounds

Unhealed wounds distort identity.□
They shape how we see ourselves, how we interpret other people's actions, and even how we perceive God.

A wound of rejection can make every "no" feel like proof you're unlovable.

A wound of abandonment can make you cling to people who treat you badly just so you're not alone.

A wound of betrayal can make trust feel impossible, even with those who've never hurt you.

Left untreated, these wounds start writing our story for us. They determine the relationships we choose, the risks we take (or avoid), and the level of joy we allow ourselves to experience.

My Father, The Connection, and the Quiet Wound that Lay Dormant

April 2011 was one of the most surreal days of my life. I was heading to Suffolk County, NY, to meet my biological father for the first time. The man whose absence had shaped so much of my story was suddenly going to be standing in front of me.

When we met, I saw my own features in his face. My first words to him were, "Dad, more than anything in my life, I just wanted to know you. I have no hate in my heart towards you."

That was the truth. I had no time to waste because, ideally, this was a moment I wasn't going to take for granted. Here I was, finally meeting the man I had long awaited — but that was also only part of my truth. Because at that time, beneath those words, was a wound I had been managing for years without ever letting God fully treat it. I thought forgiving him was the same thing as being healed. But forgiveness is the first step — not the final one.

To this day, my father and I are locked in like peas in a pod. But even though the relationship is solid, there are still some kinks as a man that I daily work out—areas where I needed God to help me through.

It took time, intentionality, and vulnerability to let God go deeper — to let Him deal not just with the facts of my father's absence and the "now" moment of us meeting, but with the identity lies I had believed because of what the wound had birthed in me.

The Deception of Surface Healing

Here's the danger: wounds can look healed on the outside while still rotting inside.□
A smile, a polished social media feed, a well-delivered sermon — none of these are proof that the infection is gone.

We can deceive ourselves into thinking that because the bleeding has stopped, the healing is done. But surface healing is fragile. One trigger, one comment, one rejection can rip the wound wide open again.

That's why God's healing process often feels invasive. He doesn't just want to close the wound; He wants to clean it out so it doesn't return. That can mean reopening old pain, revisiting hard memories, and dismantling the false coping mechanisms we've built.

God's Prescription for Wounded Souls

Psalm 147:3 says:
"He heals the brokenhearted and binds up their wounds." (NIV)

Notice the order: healing first, then binding. God doesn't just wrap up the injury to make it look better — He heals it from the inside out.□
The process can include:

Revelation – God showing you the real root of the wound.

Repentance – Turning away from the patterns that kept the wound alive.

Restoration – Receiving the truth about who you are in Christ, which replaces the lies the wound told you.

Why We Resist the Process

We resist deep healing for the same reason we keep masks on — it's uncomfortable. It means sitting in the pain long enough for God to work. It means giving up the illusion of control.□
But here's the truth: refusing to deal with the wound doesn't make it go away — it just makes it worse.

Proverbs 28:13 (AMP) says:
"He who conceals his transgressions will not prosper, but whoever confesses and turns away from his sins will find compassion and mercy."

That principle applies not just to sin, but to wounds. Concealment prevents prosperity — not just financially, but in every area of life.

From Wounded to Whole

Wholeness isn't about having no scars — it's about having scars that no longer bleed.

When I think about my father now, there's no sting. The wound has become a testimony. It's proof of God's ability to restore what was broken. But getting here required surrender — not just once, but over and over, as God brought deeper layers of the wound to the surface.

The work of dealing with the wound is ongoing. But every time you let God clean out another layer, the infection loses more of its power, and the deception loses more of its hold.

The secret deception is that you can live a full life without dealing with the wound. The truth is, you can't. The wound will show up in your words, your habits, your relationships, and your faith — until you let God heal it completely.

Taking off the mask was the first step. Letting God treat the injury is the next. And once He begins that process, you'll find yourself at what I call *The Awakening Point* — the moment when you finally come to grips with yourself, your past, and your need for lasting change.

THE AWAKENING POINT – COMING TO GRIPS WITH MYSELF

When God begins to deal with our wounds, there is a moment—sometimes gradual, sometimes explosive—where the fog starts to lift. You begin to see yourself clearly, not through the distorted lens of pain, shame, or performance, but through the unfiltered truth of who you are and where you are.

This is what I call the Awakening Point.

It's the moment when the excuses start to sound hollow, the masks no longer fit, and the old patterns begin to lose their grip. It's when you stop negotiating with dysfunction and start confronting it.

The Prodigal's Turning Point

Jesus paints this moment vividly in the parable of the prodigal son:

"But when he came to himself, he said, 'How many of my father's hired servants have bread enough and to spare, and I perish with hunger!'" (Luke 15:17, NKJV)

That phrase—"came to himself"—is more than realization. In the Greek, it carries the sense of sobering up, regaining one's senses, waking from a delusion. It's the spiritual equivalent of being shaken awake from a dangerous dream.

The son's awakening didn't erase his past, but it reframed his future. It didn't remove the mess he had made, but it reminded him of a home he could return to.

Why Awakening Feels Like a Crisis

Here's the truth: awakening often comes disguised as a crisis.

A marriage on the brink.□
A career collapse.□
A health scare.□
A moral failure exposed.

In those moments, the illusion of control shatters. And while it can feel like life is falling apart, God may actually be pulling back the curtain so you can finally see what's been broken for a long time.

William James said, "The greatest discovery of any generation is that a human can alter his life by altering his attitudes." The prodigal's circumstances didn't change in that moment—but his mindset did. And that mental shift set the stage for transformation.

My Own Awakening

I shared earlier about meeting my biological father at twenty-four, just before my twenty-fifth birthday. What I didn't share then was how much that meeting shook me awake.

For years, I had been carrying unspoken narratives about my worth, my manhood, and my future—many of them shaped by his absence. But seeing him in person forced me to confront both the truth and the lies I had believed.

It wasn't instant healing. It wasn't a Hollywood reunion scene where everything suddenly felt whole. But it was an awakening. I saw clearly how much of my identity had been shaped in reaction to pain, rather than in response to God's truth.

That realization was both liberating and terrifying. Because now I couldn't hide behind "I didn't know." I knew. And once you know, you're responsible for what you do with that knowledge.

The Mirror Moment

Awakening is like standing in front of a mirror you've been avoiding. James 1:23–25 (AMP) describes it:

"For if anyone only listens to the word without obeying it, he is like a man who looks very carefully at his natural face in a mirror; for once he has looked at himself and gone away, he immediately forgets what he looked like. But he who looks carefully into the perfect law, the law of liberty, and faithfully abides by it... will be blessed in what he does."

The Awakening Point is when you stop walking away from the mirror. You linger. You take inventory. You admit what needs to change.

And here's the crucial part—you don't just notice; you act.

The Battle of the Mind

Romans 12:2 (NLT) tells us:

"Don't copy the behavior and customs of this world, but let God transform you into a new person by changing the way you think."

The battlefield of awakening is the mind. Your external behavior will never sustainably change until your internal narrative changes.

That means:

Rejecting lies — "I'll always be this way." "I'm too far gone." "This is just who I am."

Replacing with truth — "I am a new creation in Christ" (2 Corinthians 5:17, ESV). "He who began a good work in me will carry it on to completion" (Philippians 1:6, NIV).

Reinforcing through action — making decisions that align with the new truth, even before your emotions catch up.

Why Some Resist Awakening

Not everyone embraces this moment. Some fight it. Some run from it. Why? Because awakening forces change, and change threatens comfort.

Remember, comfort zones don't require courage. Awakening does. It means breaking habits, having hard conversations, facing consequences, and surrendering pride.

It's easier to stay in the pigpen than to face the road home—because the road home is humbling. But it's also the only road to restoration.

From Awareness to Action

An awakening without action is just awareness. Awareness can make you informed; only action makes you transformed.

For the prodigal son, coming to himself meant getting up and going back to his father. For us, it might mean:

Making the counseling appointment.

Apologizing to the person we wronged.

Cutting ties with toxic influences.

Rebuilding spiritual disciplines like prayer, fasting, and Scripture study.

The Awakening Point is God's mercy giving us a choice: stay as you are, or step into what you were meant to be.

The Reward of Awakening

When you respond to awakening with obedience, you step into a different kind of life. Not a perfect life, but a purposeful one.

And here's the beautiful paradox: awakening doesn't make you flawless—it makes you faithful. It turns your limp into a testimony, your scar into a story, your past into a platform for God's glory.

Coming to grips with yourself is not about condemnation—it's about liberation. It's about finally telling the truth about where you are so God can lead you to where you need to be.

Once you've had that awakening moment, you're ready for what comes next: walking in healing with a new identity. And that's where we meet Jacob—wounded, renamed, and forever changed.

Which takes us to Chapter 7 – "Healed, Filled, and Name Changed! But the Wound Serves as a Reminder!"—the place where victory and vulnerability meet.

HEALED, FILLED, AND NAME CHANGED!

(BUT THE WOUND SERVES AS A REMINDER!)

Healing in God's Kingdom is not a cosmetic fix—it's a complete renovation. When God heals you, He doesn't just patch the cracks; He transforms the foundation. But here's the paradox that many don't understand: God can heal you completely and still leave a scar. Sometimes, He even leaves a limp.

Not because the healing was incomplete, but because the reminder is necessary. The reminder protects you from pride, keeps you dependent on Him, and becomes the testimony that speaks to others still in their struggle.

The Night Jacob Wrestled

Genesis 32:24–28 (NLT) gives us one of the most dramatic personal encounters with God recorded in Scripture:

"This left Jacob all alone in the camp, and a man came and wrestled with him until the dawn began to break. When the man saw that he would not win the match, he touched Jacob's hip and wrenched it out of its socket. Then the man said, 'Let me go, for the dawn is breaking!'

But Jacob said, 'I will not let you go unless you bless me.'

'What is your name?' the man asked.

He replied, 'Jacob.'

'Your name will no longer be Jacob,' the man told him. 'From now on you will be called Israel, because you have fought with God and with men and have won.'"

Jacob walked away with two things: a blessing and a limp. The blessing marked his new identity; the limp marked the encounter that changed him.

The Wound That Blesses

When you truly encounter God, something in you changes forever. That change is often two-fold:

An internal transformation—new identity, renewed mind, restored purpose.

An external reminder—something visible, tangible, or experiential that points back to that transformation.

For Jacob, it was the limp. For Paul, it was the "thorn in the flesh" (2 Corinthians 12:7–9). For you and me, it might be a scar, a memory, a limitation, or a vulnerability we never fully shake in this life.

The reminder isn't punishment—it's preservation.

Why God Leaves the Limp

In the natural, we see wounds as weaknesses to be hidden. In the Kingdom, God often uses them as witness tools.

Paul understood this. He wrote:

"Each time he said, 'My grace is all you need. My power works best in weakness.' So now I am glad to boast about my weaknesses, so that the power of Christ can work through me." (2 Corinthians 12:9, NLT)

When God leaves a limp, He's making sure you never forget where your strength comes from. That way, when people see your progress, you can't take the credit.

From Striver to Surrendered

Jacob's old name meant "supplanter," "schemer," or "heel-grabber"—a man who got ahead by manipulation. But after wrestling with God, he walked away as Israel—"God strives" or "one who has wrestled with God."

The shift wasn't just semantic; it was spiritual. Jacob's striving was replaced by God's sovereignty. His identity was no longer rooted in his cunning, but in God's covenant.

And yet, the limp remained. It was as if God said, "You will walk into your future blessed, but you will never forget the night you stopped fighting Me and started surrendering to Me."

My Limp, My Lesson

I've learned that my own "limps"—the things I wish I could erase from my story—are actually the very things God uses most powerfully.

The absence of my father, the seasons of masking pain, the wounds I carried for years—I wouldn't have chosen any of them. But now, I wouldn't erase them either.

Because every time I feel the ache of those memories, I'm reminded:
God met me there.
God changed me there.
God blessed me there.

Living Healed, Not Hiding the Scar

Too many believers treat their healing like a cover-up—as if the goal is to act like the wound never happened. But real healing doesn't erase history; it redeems it.

In John 20:27 (NASB), Jesus invites Thomas to:

"Reach here with your finger, and see My hands; and reach here your hand and put it into My side; and do not be unbelieving, but believing."

Even in His resurrected body, Jesus kept His scars. Why? Because the scars told the story of victory. They were evidence that death had been defeated.

In the same way, your scars are not liabilities; they are receipts. They prove the debt has been paid.

Psychology of the Reminder

From a psychological perspective, a physical or emotional reminder of past pain can be both grounding and guiding.

Grounding: It keeps you from drifting back into arrogance or self-reliance.

Guiding: It helps you recognize danger signs early, so you don't repeat destructive patterns.

When handled with humility, reminders can protect you. When handled with shame, they can paralyze you. The difference is whether you see them through the lens of redemption or regret.

The Power of a Renamed Life

Revelation 2:17 (ESV) says,

"To the one who conquers... I will give him a white stone, with a new name written on the stone that no one knows except the one who receives it."

God is in the business of giving new names. He renamed Abram to Abraham, Sarai to Sarah, Simon to Peter, Saul to Paul. The name change signifies identity change, and identity change signifies destiny change.

But here's the catch—the name change doesn't erase the journey that led there.

To be healed is to be made whole. To be filled is to walk in the fullness of the Spirit. To be renamed is to step into your God-given identity. But to keep the reminder is to remain anchored in gratitude and humility.

The limp isn't a curse; it's a compass. It points you back to the place where God met you, changed you, and marked you forever.

And when you embrace the limp, you're ready for what comes next—moving into a new life where your past no longer defines you, but your testimony refines you.

Which takes us into **Chapter 8 – "The Awakening Expanded – Living Beyond the Moment"**—learning to sustain what God has started.

THE AWAKENING: LIVING BEYOND THE MOMENT

An awakening moment is powerful, but it's only the beginning. Just like a wedding day launches a marriage, your awakening is meant to launch a lifestyle. The danger is thinking that because you felt changed in a moment, you'll stay changed without effort.

The truth is, transformation must be cultivated.

It's not just about what God did in a flash of revelation—it's about what you choose to do every day afterward.

From Encounter to Endurance

Jacob's limp was a daily reminder of his encounter, but if all he did was reminisce about that night at Peniel, nothing in his life would have changed. The limp had to inform his walk, not just his memory.

The same is true for us. The high of an awakening moment will fade—not because God's presence diminishes, but because life has a way of testing whether that moment became a conviction or stayed a feeling.

James 1:25 (ESV) says:

"But the one who looks into the perfect law, the law of liberty, and perseveres... will be blessed in his doing."

Notice that word: *perseveres*. Awakening may start with a sudden lightbulb, but living beyond it requires the grit to keep going when the glow fades.

Biblical Examples of Sustained Awakening

Joshua After Jericho – The walls fell miraculously, but Joshua still had to lead the people through countless battles afterward. Victory in one moment did not exempt him from daily obedience.

Peter After Pentecost – The fire fell, the Spirit filled, and thousands were saved in a single day. But Peter's ministry was forged in the grind of prayer meetings, persecution, and preaching the same gospel to hostile crowds over and over again.

Paul After Damascus – The blinding light and voice of Jesus changed his direction, but Paul still spent years learning, teaching, traveling, and enduring hardship to walk out what started on that road.

These men remind us: A God-moment is meant to start a God-movement in your life.

The Psychology of Keeping Change

Psychologists tell us that change is most likely to last when it becomes embedded in our identity, not just our behavior. In other words, the question shifts from "What do I need to do?" to "Who am I now?"

If you see yourself as someone *trying* to pray, you'll pray inconsistently.□
If you see yourself as a *prayerful person*, prayer becomes part of your natural rhythm.

Romans 12:2 (MSG) puts it beautifully:

"Fix your attention on God. You'll be changed from the inside out... Readily recognize what he wants from you and quickly respond to it."

Sustained awakening is about aligning your identity with your new reality in Christ.

My Post-Awakening Struggle

I remember a season after a major spiritual breakthrough when I thought I had "arrived." I was preaching, serving, and in my Bible more than ever. But slowly, I started coasting—thinking the momentum would carry me without intentionality.

It didn't.

The old patterns didn't just disappear; they waited for my guard to drop.□ That's when I realized: God's grace will save you in a moment, but it will train you over a lifetime (Titus 2:11–12). Without the training, you will drift back to where you were, no matter how powerful your awakening felt.

Spiritual Disciplines That Sustain Awakening

To live beyond the moment, you must anchor your life in rhythms that keep you connected to God's presence and truth.

Daily Word Immersion – Not just reading for information, but meditating for transformation (Psalm 1:2–3).

Consistent Prayer – Conversation with God as a lifestyle, not an event (1 Thessalonians 5:17).

Community Accountability – Surrounding yourself with people who challenge and encourage you (Hebrews 10:24–25).

Worship as Warfare – Praising God not only in the sanctuary but in the storm (2 Chronicles 20:22).

Obedience in the Small Things – Faithfulness in what seems insignificant is what qualifies you for greater (Luke 16:10).

Guardrails for Your New Life

Living beyond the moment also means building boundaries that protect your progress. For some, that might mean changing environments; for others, it's ending toxic relationships or limiting influences that trigger old habits.

Proverbs 4:23 (NLT) says:
"Guard your heart above all else, for it determines the course of your life."

Guarding your heart isn't paranoia—it's stewardship.

From Emotional to Eternal

The awakening moment is often emotional—tears, joy, relief. But sustained transformation must move from emotional to eternal. That means you stop measuring your growth by how you feel and start measuring it by how you faithfully obey, even when emotions aren't high.

Awakening is God's gift; sustaining it is your stewardship. The moment opens your eyes, but the movement keeps you walking in the light.

Living beyond the moment is about building a life that your awakening prepared you for—a life where your limp, your scars, and your testimony all point to the same truth: God started this work, and He will finish it.

And now, we come to **Chapter 9 – "Shalom: The Full Circle of Wholeness"**—the destination where the mask is gone, the wound is healed, the identity is secure, and the life of peace in God becomes your new normal.

SHALOM

When I think about everything we've walked through—the masks, the wounds, the awakening, the limp, and the new identity—there is one word that rises above them all: Shalom.

Shalom is not the absence of conflict. It is not simply "peace" in the way the English language has flattened the word. In the Hebrew, *shalom* is a vast, rich concept. It means wholeness, completeness, safety, harmony, welfare, tranquility, prosperity, and restoration. It speaks to every layer of human existence—spirit, soul, and body.

The Garden Before the Fall

To understand Shalom, we have to go back to the Garden of Eden. In Genesis 2, Adam and Eve lived in perfect harmony—with God, with each other, and within themselves. There was no shame, no striving, no insecurity, no fear. This was Shalom in its purest form—life as God intended.

But when sin entered, Shalom shattered. The relationship with God fractured. Harmony between man and woman broke. Peace within themselves gave way to hiding, blame, and toil.

Since that day, humanity has been trying to piece Shalom back together—but the truth is, Shalom can't be manufactured. It's not something we create; it's something we receive from the One who is Peace Himself (Ephesians 2:14).

Shalom in the Storm

Jesus lived and moved in Shalom even when His surroundings were chaotic. In Mark 4:39 (NASB), we read:

"And He got up and rebuked the wind and said to the sea, 'Hush, be still.' And the wind died down and it became perfectly calm."

The same voice that brought calm to the storm on the sea brings calm to the storm within us. That's why Jesus could promise in John 14:27 (NLT):

"I am leaving you with a gift—peace of mind and heart. And the peace I give is a gift the world cannot give. So don't be troubled or afraid."

Shalom doesn't mean storms won't come. It means the storm doesn't get the final word.

My Journey into Shalom

- Looking back, I can see that every stage of my healing was leading me here:

- Removing the mask (authenticity).

- Addressing the wound (healing).

- Facing the truth (awakening).

- Accepting the limp (humility).

- Living beyond the moment (discipline).

Shalom is the gift on the other side of surrender. It's waking up in the morning without the weight of pretending. It's being at peace with who you are because you know Whose you are. It's walking through challenges with a quiet confidence that God's got it—and you.

The Layers of Shalom

Peace with God – This is the foundation. Romans 5:1 (NIV) says, "Therefore, since we have been justified through faith, we have peace with God through our Lord Jesus Christ." No more running. No more hiding. You are reconciled.

Peace within Yourself – The internal war ends when you align your thoughts with God's truth. Isaiah 26:3 (ESV) promises, "You keep him in perfect peace whose mind is stayed on you, because he trusts in you."

Peace with Others – Shalom flows outward. Matthew 5:9 (NLT) declares, "God blesses those who work for peace, for they will be called the children of God."

Living Shalom Daily

Shalom is not a one-time deposit; it's a daily walk.

Guard Your Mind – What you dwell on determines your peace level (Philippians 4:8).

Release Control – Shalom thrives in surrender, not in micromanagement (Proverbs 3:5–6).

Stay Rooted in the Word – Scripture is the anchor in a restless world (Psalm 119:165).

Practice Gratitude – Gratitude magnifies what God is doing rather than what's missing (1 Thessalonians 5:18).

The Final Full Circle

In the beginning, man's Shalom was stolen in a garden. In the end, Revelation 21–22 paints a picture of Shalom fully restored—God dwelling with His people, every tear wiped away, no more death, mourning, crying, or pain.

We live in the tension between Eden lost and Eden restored. And yet, in Christ, we can taste Shalom now—not perfectly, but truly.

Epilogue

If you've read this far, it's because something in you is hungry for more than survival. You want wholeness. You want the fullness of God's peace in every area of your life.

Here's the good news: It's already yours in Christ. The same God who met Jacob in the dark, who calmed the storm for the disciples, who gave His life to reconcile you to the Father—He is the God who will walk you into Shalom and keep you there.

So walk forward. Limp if you must. But walk in Shalom. And let your healed wounds, your honest story, and your renewed identity be the testimony that points others toward the same peace you've found.

Because this isn't just the end of a book—it's the beginning of a new way of living.

The Void Filler Workbook Companion Chapters 1–9

By Damon L. Morgan

Workbook Edition | For Personal and Group Study

Now that you have made it to this point, let's actually walk this out together. I have compiled a comprehensive workbook plan for you to use as a tool to aid in identifying the things in your life that could be the VOID and how to work through those different phases. Though I can't physically be with you, utilize the imagery of the book as a metaphor for me holding your hand. The work may be challenging, annoying, or frustrating, but it's totally worth the process.

The Void Filler - Workbook Companion (Chapters 1–4)

This workbook companion is designed to walk alongside you as you journey through *The Void Filler.* It contains Scripture focus points, summaries, reflection questions, action steps, and prayer prompts to help you apply the truths of each chapter in practical, life-changing ways.

Chapter 1 – It Starts Somewhere...

Key Scripture Focus

- Philippians 1:6 (NLT)

- Zechariah 4:10 (NLT)

- Psalm 37:23 (NASB)

- Genesis 3:1 (ESV)

- Ecclesiastes 3:11 (NLT)

- Romans 3:23 (NASB)

- Jeremiah 17:9 (KJV)

- Romans 7 (Message)

Summary Point

Every journey of restoration begins with a moment of recognition—a realization that something sacred has been lost. Whether it started in a garden, a childhood wound, or a quiet ache, the void within us points to a deeper longing for wholeness. This chapter invites us to acknowledge the ache, not with shame, but with hope—because what begins in brokenness can be redeemed by the One who fills the void with His presence.

Reflection Questions

What is one moment in your life that awakened a deeper awareness of your need for God?

_____

_____

How have you experienced the 'displacement ache'—that sense of something missing—in your own story?

_____

_____

What are some ways you've tried to fill the void in your heart? Have they satisfied?

_____

_____

Who in your life holds you accountable when you begin to drift from truth?

_____

_____

What would it look like to invite God into the very place where you feel most empty?

_____

_____

Action Steps

☐ **Name the void.** Write down one area of your life where you feel a persistent ache or emptiness.

☐ **Identify.** Note one way you've tried to fill that void apart from God, and surrender it in prayer.

☐ **Reach out.** Contact a trusted friend or mentor and invite them to walk with you in accountability.

☐ **Pursue.** Choose one intentional step this week to pursue God's presence in that area—through prayer, Scripture, or silence.

Prayer Prompt

Lord, I recognize the ache within me—the void that nothing in this world can fill. Forgive me for the ways I've tried to silence it with substitutes. I invite You into that space. Fill me with Your presence, restore what has been lost, and lead me on the path of healing. Help me to trust that even in my brokenness, You are beginning something beautiful. Amen.

Chapter 2 – Removing the Mask

Key Scripture Focus

- 2 Corinthians 3:13, 16 (ESV)

- Psalm 51:6 (NIV)

- Proverbs 11:3 (ESV)

Summary Point

Masks protect us from exposure but also keep us from true intimacy with God and others. Real transformation begins when we allow ourselves to be fully seen and fully loved.

Reflection Questions

What 'masks' have you worn to hide your true self from others or from God?

_____

_____

In what situations do you feel most tempted to hide behind a façade?

_____

_____

How has masking your pain or struggles affected your relationships?

_____

_____

What would it look like to live with greater transparency in your walk with God and others?

_____

Action Steps

☐ Identify one area of your life where you've been hiding and bring it honestly before God in prayer.

☐ Invite a trusted believer to walk with you in accountability as you remove the mask.

☐ Practice vulnerability this week in at least one conversation by sharing something real instead of giving a "safe" answer.

> ### Prayer Prompt
> *Lord, You see through every mask I've ever worn. Give me the courage to lay them down and live openly before You and before those You've placed in my life. Help me to trust that Your grace is big enough to cover the real me—the me without filters or pretenses. Amen.*

Chapter 3 – The Wound

Key Scripture Focus

- Psalm 147:3 (NIV)

- Isaiah 61:1 (NIV)

- Isaiah 53:5 (NIV)

Summary Point
Wounds left unhealed can shape how we see ourselves, others, and even God. Healing is possible, but it requires honesty, surrender, and a willingness to let the Great Physician do the work.

Reflection Questions

What past wound still influences the way you think or behave today?

_____

_____

How have you tried to cope with pain apart from God's healing?

_____

_____

In what ways has holding on to hurt prevented you from moving forward?

_____

_____

How do you think God wants to use your healing to bring hope to others?

_____

_____

Action Steps

☐ Journal about one wound you have carried for a long time—be honest and specific.

☐ Invite God into that specific hurt through prayer and Scripture meditation.

☐ Seek wise counsel or pastoral care if the wound feels too heavy to face alone.

Chapter 4 – This Smile Is Hurting Me

Key Scripture Focus

- James 1:22–24 (KJV)

- Psalm 34:18 (NLT)

- 1 Samuel 16:7b (NIV)

Summary Point

Sometimes the biggest smiles hide the deepest pain. True healing begins when we stop pretending and allow God to deal with what's behind the mask of happiness.

Reflection Questions

Have you ever worn a "smile" to cover up pain? What was really going on inside?

_____

_____

What fears keep you from letting others see your true emotional state?

_____

_____

How can acknowledging your pain in God's presence be a step toward healing?

_____

_____

Who in your life could you trust to see beyond your smile and walk with you through the pain?

_____

_____

Action Steps

☐ Pause this week and honestly assess your emotional state—write down what you're really feeling.

☐ Pray daily for God to align your outward expression with inward truth.

☐ Choose one person to share something you've been hiding behind a smile.

Prayer Prompt

Lord, You see behind every smile I wear. You know the weight I carry and the tears I've held back. I invite You into the hidden places of my heart. Help me to drop the act, trust Your love, and live in a way that my joy is rooted in You, not in pretending I'm okay. Amen.

The Void Filler - Workbook Companion (Chapters 5–9)

This workbook companion continues to walk alongside you as you journey through *The Void Filler*. It contains Scripture focus points, summaries, reflection questions, action steps, and prayer prompts for Chapters 5–9, helping you apply the truths of each chapter in practical, life-changing ways.

Chapter 5 – Dealing with the Wounds: The Secret Deception

Key Scripture Focus

- Hebrews 4:13 (NIV)

- John 8:32 (CSB)

- James 5:16a (NASB)

Summary Point
Hiding wounds may feel like self-protection, but secrecy can become a prison. God invites us into the light, where truth dismantles deception and begins the work of real healing.

Reflection Questions

What "secret" hurt have you tried to keep from others or even from God?

_____

_____

How has hiding this wound affected your spiritual growth?

_____

_____

Why do you think secrecy can make a wound even more painful?

_____

_____

What steps could you take this week to bring one hidden hurt into the light?

_____

_____

Action Steps

☐ Write down the wound you've hidden the most—even if you don't share it yet, name it before God.

☐ Find a trusted, mature believer to confide in and pray with about your struggle.

☐ Commit to one practical step that moves you toward truth and away from isolation.

Prayer Prompt

Father, You already know the hurt I've been hiding. I confess that I've kept it in the dark out of fear and shame. But I want to be free. Give me courage to bring my pain into the light and to trust that Your grace is big enough to cover it. Heal me as I walk in truth. Amen.

Chapter 6 – The Awakening: Coming to Grips with Myself

Key Scripture Focus

- Luke 15:17 (NIV)

- Psalm 139:23–24 (NLT)

- 2 Corinthians 13:5a (CSB)

Summary Point

The awakening moment is when you finally see yourself clearly in light of God's truth. It's the turning point where denial ends, honesty begins, and transformation becomes possible.

Reflection Questions

When have you had a "come to your senses" moment in your walk with God?

_____

_____

What truths about yourself has God been trying to show you recently?

_____

_____

Why is self-examination essential to spiritual growth?

_____

_____

What areas of your life still resist God's correction?

_____

_____

Action Steps

☐ Spend 15 minutes in prayer asking God to reveal blind spots in your heart.

☐ Write down one truth about yourself that's hard to face but necessary for growth.

☐Plan one concrete change you can make this week in response to God's prompting.

Prayer Prompt

Lord, thank You for the moments when You open my eyes to see myself as I really am. Even when the truth is hard, help me embrace it knowing that Your correction is an act of love. Lead me into the changes that will bring me closer to You and more in line with Your will. Amen.

Chapter 7 – Healed, Filled, and Name Changed! (But the Wound Serves as a Reminder)

Key Scripture Focus

- Genesis 32:28 (NIV)

- 2 Corinthians 12:9a (NIV)

- Isaiah 49:16 (NIV)

Summary Point
God's healing often changes our identity and fills us with new purpose.
But He sometimes leaves a visible reminder—not as a punishment, but as a testimony to His power and faithfulness.

Reflection Questions

When has God transformed your identity or sense of purpose?

How can you see your past wounds as reminders of His faithfulness rather than signs of failure?

_____

_____

What "limp" has God allowed to remain in your life, and how does it keep you dependent on Him?

_____

_____

How can you use your testimony to encourage others still in the struggle?

_____

_____

Action Steps

☐ Write down how God has changed your identity in Him—old labels vs. new ones.

☐ Share a part of your testimony with someone who needs hope this week.

☐ Thank God specifically for the ways your "limp" has protected you from pride or self-reliance.

Chapter 8 – The Awakening Expanded: Living Beyond the Moment

Key Scripture Focus

- Galatians 6:9 (NIV)

- Colossians 2:6–7a (ESV)

- Philippians 3:14 (NIV)

Summary Point

A spiritual awakening isn't just a one-time high—it's an invitation to a sustained walk of obedience. The goal is to carry transformation forward into everyday life so the moment becomes a movement.

Reflection Questions

Have you experienced a spiritual "high" that was hard to maintain afterward? What happened?

_____

_____

What daily habits help you remain close to God after powerful encounters with Him?

_____

How do you keep your focus when spiritual growth feels slow or challenging?

_____

_____

What does "living beyond the moment" look like for you right now?

_____

_____

Action Steps

☐ Identify one spiritual discipline you can strengthen this week (prayer, Scripture study, fasting, worship).

☐ Set a realistic daily or weekly goal for maintaining your spiritual momentum.

☐ Invite someone to hold you accountable in living out your renewed commitment.

Prayer Prompt

Lord, thank You for the moments when You awaken my heart to Your presence in a powerful way. Help me to live faithfully beyond the mountaintop experiences, carrying the lessons and commitments into my daily walk. Keep me rooted in You so my transformation endures. Amen.

Chapter 9 – Shalom

Key Scripture Focus

- Isaiah 26:3 (NIV)

- John 14:27 (NIV)

- Psalm 29:11 (NIV)

Summary Point

Shalom is more than the absence of conflict—it is God's gift of wholeness, completeness, and harmony in every part of life. It is both a present reality in Christ and a future promise in God's eternal kingdom.

Reflection Questions

What does "Shalom" mean to you after reading this chapter?

_____

_____

In what areas of your life do you most need God's wholeness right now?

_____

_____

How does knowing Shalom is a gift from God (and not self-made) change the way you pursue it?

_____

_____

Who in your life could benefit from seeing God's peace lived out through you?

_____

_____

Action Steps

☐ Spend five minutes each morning meditating on one Scripture about peace.

☐ Ask God to show you one way you can be a peacemaker in your relationships this week.

☐ Write a short testimony of how God has brought peace into your life, and be ready to share it when He opens the door.

Prayer Prompt

Prince of Peace, thank You for the gift of Shalom—wholeness that comes from You alone. Teach me to live in Your peace daily, to guard it from distraction, and to extend it to those around me. Keep me rooted in Your presence until the day when perfect Shalom is fully restored in Your kingdom. Amen.

SALVATION OFFERING!

As alluded to in the book—THERE ARE MANY REASONS WHY WE GET THROWN OFF TRACK! BUT THERE IS HOPE IN CHRIST THAT IF WE LAY DOWN:

OUR IDOLS

OUR FAILURES

OUR CHILDHOOD TRAUMA (Learned behavior and generational habits)

BROKEN RELATIONSHIPS

DIVORCE

SEPARATION

BEREAVEMENT TRAUMA

OUR POOR DECISIONS (Self-inflictions)

HE WILL IN TURN COME AND FILL US. THE RESPONSE ON OUR PART IS TAKING AN INTROSPECTIVE APPROACH: LOOKING AT WHERE WE USED TO BE AND NOW LOOKING AT WHERE WE ARE BECAUSE OF HIM!

If you want to rededicate your life to CHRIST—Here's YOUR Opportunity!

Lord Jesus, I confess my sins and ask for Your forgiveness. Please come into my heart as my Lord and Savior. Take complete control of my life and help me to walk in Your footsteps as Your Holy Spirit leads me. Fill up the voids and wounds from life that have happened to me and that I caused! I accept Your love and fellowship! I AFFIRM MY FAITH IN YOU and I AM FILLED WITH YOUR SPIRIT!

Romans 10:9-10 says:

9 That if you confess with your mouth, "Jesus is Lord," and believe in your heart that God raised Him from the dead, you will be saved.□
10 For with your heart you believe and are justified, and with your mouth you confess and are saved.

Remember this... Only Jesus can truly satisfy your soul. By Him filling "EVERY VOID," He will without a doubt make you WHOLE and COMPLETE! I challenge you, upon your completion of this book—Try Him! He has a guarantee that with Him all things will be well! Trust me, I am living proof! PURSUE SHALOM!

Until next time!

About the author

Damon L. Morgan is a Bronx, New York native born in the 1980s, shaped by the grit, resilience, and cultural richness of his upbringing. He is a devoted husband, proud father of three, uncle, son, grandson, and a minister of the Gospel—roles that anchor his life and inform his calling.

Raised in an environment that demanded perseverance, Damon carries that same resolve into his faith and mission, pursuing a life marked by growth, service, and transformation.

A passionate lover and disciple of Jesus Christ, Damon is committed to sharing the message of Christ until all have heard. His life's work is rooted in seeing lives changed—one day, one moment, and one encounter at a time.

In this reflective memoir, Damon invites readers into his most authentic self, chronicling a journey from personal struggle to spiritual victory. This book stands as a testament to the power of Christ-centered living and the transformative beauty of a genuine relationship with God. Through transparency, faith, and hope, Damon challenges readers to explore what it truly means to live in **shalom**—a life of wholeness, peace, and divine purpose.

www.ingramcontent.com/pod-product-compliance
Lightning Source LLC
Chambersburg PA
CBHW061712120626
46550CB00003B/1196